D0924604

10 Fascinating Facts About

by Rachel Grack

Content Consultant

David Shiffman, Research Assistant
University of Miami

Reading Consultant

Jeanne M. Clidas, Ph.D.
Reading Specialist

Children's Press®
An Imprint of Scholastic Inc.

Table of Contents

There are more than 500 **species** of sharks. These fish swim in waters around the world. Sharks can be shorter than a ruler or longer than a bus. They are strong and fast. They are some of the most fearsome **predators** on Earth.

Do you want to learn more fascinating facts about sharks? Then read on!

Shark skin can bite

Denticles help a shark swim quickly and quietly.

A shark's skin is covered in **denticles**. These scales are a little like teeth. If you were to run your hand down a shark's back, the

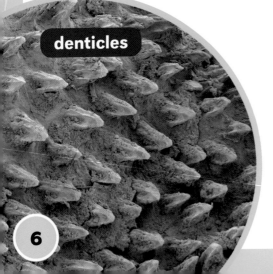

denticles

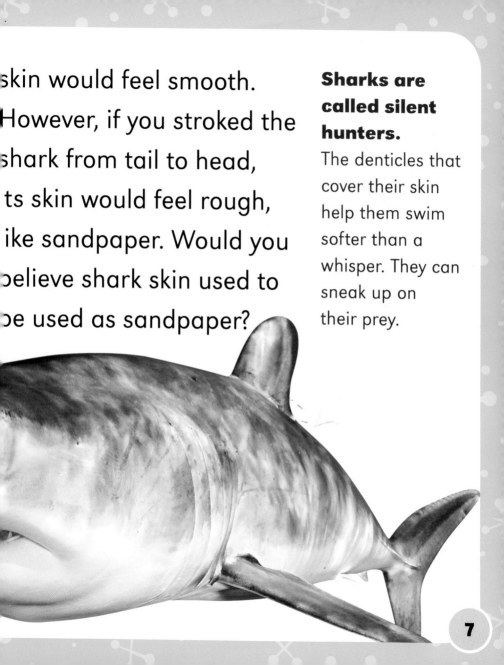

skin would feel smooth. However, if you stroked the shark from tail to head, its skin would feel rough, like sandpaper. Would you believe shark skin used to be used as sandpaper?

Sharks are called silent hunters.

The denticles that cover their skin help them swim softer than a whisper. They can sneak up on their prey.

7

These fish are boneless

This cutaway image shows a shark's gills (1), skeleton (2), and some organs (3).

Shark skeletons are made of cartilage and muscle. Cartilage is the same material that makes

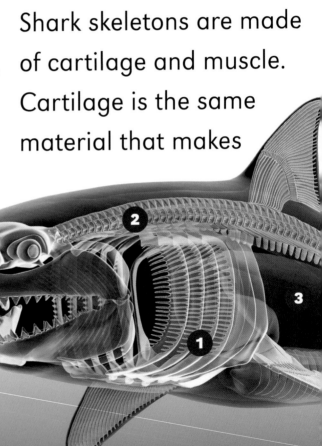

The velvet belly lantern shark is only 18 inches (46 centimeters) long. It is one of the smallest sharks in the world.

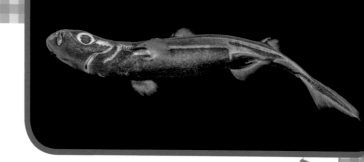

the hard parts of your nose and ears. It is lighter and more flexible than regular bone. Lightweight skeletons keep sharks from sinking.

Velvet belly lantern sharks have glow-in-the-dark spines. They look sort of like an X-ray. The way the spines glow serves as a warning sign to predators. They are much too sharp to eat!

Some species seem like they can fly

Underwater, these fish move like airplanes.
A shark swims forward by swooshing its tail back and

A shark moves its tail back and forth to move through the water.

orth. Water glides over and under its fins. This movement gives the shark lift. Great white sharks jump almost 10 feet (3 meters) in the air to catch seals. This is called breaching.

Great white sharks are acrobats. Often, they do a cartwheel as they launch out of the water. Much of this shark's massive weight is at the front of its body. Its tail end flips over as it sails through the air.

Sharks pop their jaws to eat

A shark's jaw is only loosely attached to its skull. This lets sharks deliver a

A shark's jaw moves forward as it grabs a fish.

deadly surprise. They can suddenly push out their teeth to snatch passing **prey**. Their tricky jaws take one powerful bite!

Some sharks have the strongest bite of any fish. Pound for pound, bull sharks have the strongest bite of all sharks.

This predator goes through lots of teeth

A great white shark has rows of razor-sharp teeth.

A shark's teeth can quickly become dull. They often get broken. Luckily, sharks

A cookiecutter shark
left a telltale mark
on this dolphin.

have teeth to spare.
In fact, many have five
rows of teeth. Some species
replace their teeth every
10 days. A shark can lose
more than 30,000 teeth
in its life.

**Shark teeth—
and bites—**
come in many
shapes and sizes.
Some teeth are
thin and sharp.
Others are
wide and have
jagged edges.
A cookiecutter
shark attaches
like a suction
cup to its prey.
Then it takes a
circular bite!

Sharks have super senses

It is easy to see the nostrils on this lemon shark.

Some sharks can detect a tiny drop of blood in the water. Blood tells a shark an animal might be hurt. A wounded fish could

become an easy meal.
Sharks can also track the
sound of prey from up
to 650 feet (200 meters)
away. That is almost
the length of two
football fields!

**Sharks have
an extra sense
organ called**
a lateral line.
It runs down
each side of
the shark's body.
It picks up tiny
movements in
the water.
That helps the
shark find prey.

**Hammerheads
can practically
see all around
them. They have
only two blind
spots: in front of
the snout, and
right behind
the head.**

Sharks get a charge from electricity

Special organs that sense electricity look like dark spots on the underside of the shark's snout.

All living creatures give off electrical pulses. Sharks can sense this type of electricity. They have

pecial organs that can
eel the tiniest pulses.
Hundreds of these
organs line a
shark's snout.
Sharks can even
sense pulses from
creatures buried in the
ocean floor.

Sharks definitely notice when someone takes a picture underwater. Beware: Sharks sometimes mistake underwater cameras for food! Experts do not know why.

Some species never sleep

Sharks take oxygen from the water through their gills. That is how they breathe. They pump water

A great white shark has five to seven gill slits.

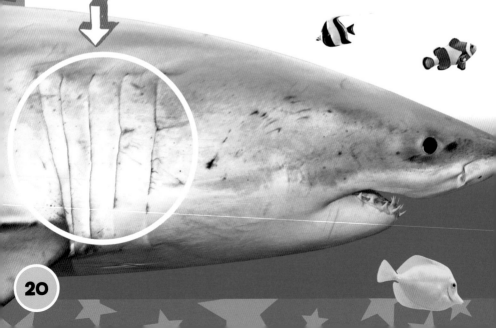

Nurse sharks can
breathe without
swimming.

over their gills while they
swim. Many sharks must
keep swimming to keep
breathing. So they never
get a truly deep sleep.

**Some sharks
have small**
openings behind
their eyes.
They are called
spiracles. The
openings let the
shark breathe
without moving.

People are not shark food

Shark attacks happen. But not because people are tasty. Usually, a shark mistakes a person for its normal meal—a seal. Every year, about

From a shark's point of view, sometimes people (1) look like turtles (2) or sea lions (3).

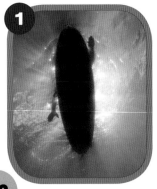

19 people in the United States are attacked. Humans are the true predators. People kill about 100 million sharks each year.

Tiger sharks eat a lot of junk! Rubber boats...license plates...car hubcaps... These are just some weird things that have ended up in sharks' bellies!

Baby sharks
are called pups

This baby shark must learn to survive on its own.

Some sharks lay eggs that hatch outside their bodies. Others grow pups inside their bodies. They give birth to live young. Some sharks even do both!

Their eggs hatch inside their bodies before the pups are born.

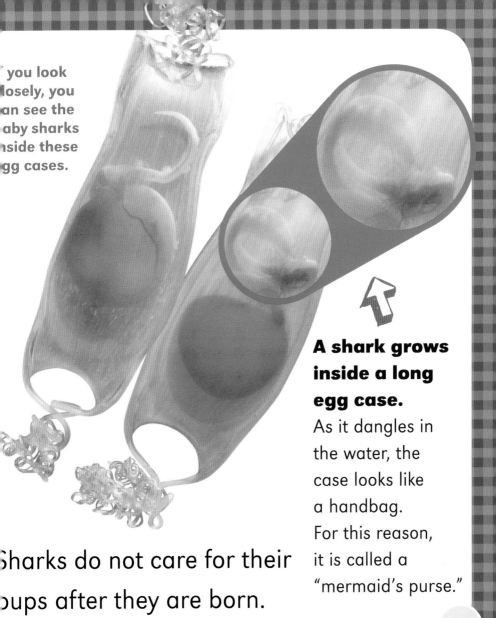

you look
losely, you
an see the
aby sharks
nside these
gg cases.

**A shark grows
inside a long
egg case.**
As it dangles in
the water, the
case looks like
a handbag.
For this reason,
it is called a
"mermaid's purse."

Sharks do not care for their
pups after they are born.

Activity

Find out how sharks stay afloat

A shark's oily liver helps it float.
This activity will show you how it works.

You Will Need:

- ✔ 2 small water bottles (empty)
- ✔ permanent markers
- ✔ cooking oil
- ✔ water
- ✔ large basin

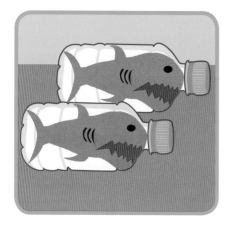

1 Draw shark faces on your water bottles.

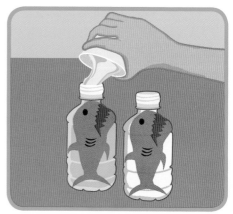

2 Fill one bottle with cooking oil. Fill the other with water.

26

3 Fill the basin with water.

4 Place both water bottles in the basin. What do you observe?

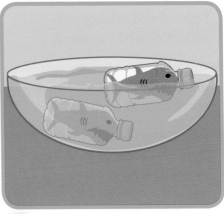

5 The cooking oil works like a real shark's oily liver—it keeps your "shark" afloat!

Super Sharks

Tiger Shark

- Tiger sharks are found in tropical and subtropical waters around the world.

- The tiger shark will eat just about anything—from fish to seabirds, and even garbage!

- This species of shark both lays eggs and gives birth to live young. The eggs hatch while still inside the female, and then live sharks are born.

Great White Shark

- The great white shark is found in all oceans except for the polar seas. It is the largest carnivorous (or meat-eating) shark in the world.

- This meat eater prefers sea lions, seals, small toothed whales, and sea turtles.

- The shark does not chew its food. It rips off chunks of meat and swallows them whole.

Whale Shark

▶ Whale sharks are found in all tropical seas.

▶ Whale sharks are the largest fish in the sea. Yet they eat the smallest creatures found there— tiny plants and animals known as plankton.

Hammerhead Shark

▶ Hammerhead sharks are found in temperate and tropical waters around the world.

▶ The hammerhead uses its wide head to trap stingrays by pinning them to the seafloor. It also eats crabs, lobsters, and squid.

Glossary

- **denticles** (DEN-tih-kuhls): toothlike scales on a shark's skin

- **predators** (PRED-uh-turs): animals that hunt other creatures for food

- **prey** (PRAY): animal that is hunted by another animal for food

- **species** (SPEE-shees): certain types of living things within a group; a great white shark is a species of shark

Index

About the Author

Rachel Grack has been writing children's nonfiction since 2001. She lives on a farm in Casa Grande, Arizona. Her favorite pastimes are enjoying her family and barnyard of animals—chickens, goats, cats, and a horse named Lady. This book is dedicated to Rachel's grandson Keaton—a ferocious appetite to learn will always lead to deep oceans of wisdom.

J
597.3
Gra

Facts for Now

Visit this Scholastic Web site for
more information on sharks:
www.factsfornow.scholastic.com
Enter the keyword **Sharks**

Library of Congress Cataloging-in-Publication Data

Names: Koestler-Grack, Rachel A., 1973– author.
Title: 10 fascinating facts about sharks/by Rachel Grack.
Other titles: Ten fascinating facts about sharks
Description: New York, NY: Children's Press, an imprint of Scholastic Inc., 2017. |
Series: Rookie star fact finder | Includes index.
Identifiers: LCCN 2016030340| ISBN 9780531222621 (library binding) |
ISBN 9780531226780 (pbk.)
Subjects: LCSH: Sharks—Juvenile literature.
Classification: LCC QL638.9 .K588 2017 | DDC 597.3—dc23
LC record available at https://lccn.loc.gov/2016030340

Produced by Spooky Cheetah Press
Design by Judith Christ-Lafond

© 2017 by Scholastic Inc.

Photographs ©: cover shark: by wildestanimal/Getty Images; cover coral reef: WaterFrame/Alamy Images; cover tropical fish and throughout: cynoclub/iStockphoto; cover background
back cover background: stock09/Shutterstock, Inc.; back cover shark: Stephen Frink Collection/Alamy Images; 3 left shark: Alexyz3d/Shutterstock, Inc.; 3 coral reef: WaterFrame/Alam
Images; 3 right shark: Stephen Frink Collection/Alamy Images; 4-5 background: Gianluca Colla/National Geographic Creative; 5 boy: Max Topchii/Shutterstock, Inc.; 6 bottom righ
The Natural History Museum/Alamy Images; 6-7 shark: Masa Ushioda/Getty Images; 8-9 shark interior: Rajeev Doshi/Getty Images; 9 top right: Espen Rekdal/Seapics.com; 10 righ
Tom Brakefield/Media Bakery; 10 left: phw/Media Bakery; 11 left: Gerard Lacz/Animals Animals; 11 center: Gerard Lacz/Animals Animals; 11 right: Gerard Lacz/Animals Animals;
Kike Calvo/National Geographic Creative; 13: Alexander Safonov/Getty Images; 14: Peter Nile/Alamy Images; 15: Stephen Frink Collection/Alamy Images; 16: Jody Watt/Getty Imag
17 coral reef: WaterFrame/Alamy Images; 17 shark: Stephen Frink Collection/Alamy Images; 18: Sascha Janson/Alamy Images; 19: by wildestanimal/Getty Images; 20: Joe Belange
Shutterstock, Inc.; 21: Yann hubert/Shutterstock, Inc.; 22 left: Chris Ross/Getty Images; 22 center: kevindickinson/Thinkstock; 22 right: NatalieJean/Shutterstock, Inc.; 23 top: Medic
Bakery; 23 bottom: Jane Rix/Shutterstock, Inc.; 24 bottom: Barcroft/Getty Images; 25: D.P. Wilson/Minden Pictures; 26-27 illustrations: Keith Plechaty; 27 girl: fatihhoca/iStockphoto;
left: Greg Amptman/Dreamstime; 28-29 illustrations: Keith Plechaty; 28 right: Alexyz3d/Shutterstock, Inc.; 29 left: Krzysztof Odziomek/Dreamstime; 29 right: Stephen Frink Collectic
Alamy Images; 30 top: The Natural History Museum/Alamy Images; 30 center top: Kike Calvo/National Geographic Creative; 30 center bottom: kevindickinson/Thinkstock; 30 botto
Media Bakery.

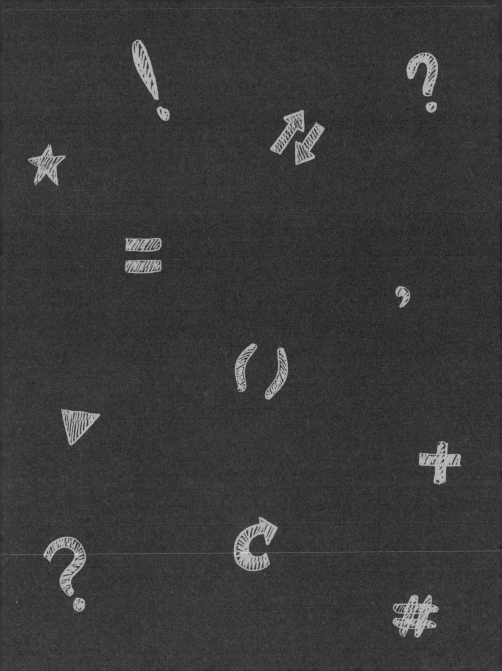